The Princess and Her Gift (Megan's Story)

Erin R. Tyler

Copyright © 2014 Erin R. Tyler
All rights reserved.
ISBN-13: 978-1494879778

ISBN-10: 1494879778

For Megan, who showed us all how to love each other more.
For Liam, who is loved more than he will ever know.

Once upon a time, there was a beautiful Princess. She was no ordinary Princess, she was intelligent and caring and strong. She always put her friends first. This beautiful Princess grew up and instead of waiting around for a prince, set out on adventures of her own. She learned as much as she could about the great big world and all the amazing things it held.

Then she set out to teach children what she had learned. She taught them all about what she had learned, took them on adventures, loved them, and gave them amazing gifts of knowledge and love and friendship.

Her life was not without challenges, but this Princess was not afraid to climb steep, rocky mountains or go through deep, dark valleys. She knew that as long as she kept up her faith and love and hope that she would be okay. Her light shined bright among her land.

One day, she learned that she would be given an amazing gift- a baby boy! Her heart was filled with joy and wonder at this gift!

But a dangerous monster came knocking at her door one day while she was still carrying this precious gift. The monster's name was Cancer.

The princess held her head high, kept her little gift safe, and used the Sword of Chemotherapy, the Shield of Radiation, and Knife of Surgery to send Cancer running.

The monster was no more. Her gift, her baby boy had arrived safely while she was fighting the monster. Her little Prince brought such joy and happiness and peace to the Princess' land. Together, they lived in their little castle and cherished every moment. They did what they knew best: loved and gave and hoped and played.

The Princess watched as her little Prince grew. She gave him as many gifts as she could, gifts of knowledge, love, and most importantly, her time. They went on wild adventures of their own, they sang songs, they played outside and explored green grasses and fresh waters.

Together, their lights shined even brighter among the Princess' land.

The Princess refused to accept defeat! She gathered her hope and love and faith around her, picked up her Sword and ran to meet the monster with all the strength that she had.

With her little Prince in her heart, she let out all of the light that she could, knowing that Light would always overcome darkness.

The little prince was safe and loved and told everyone about his beautiful and brave mother, the Princess.

To read more about Megan's courageous journey
with cancer and the gifts she left with us
please visit http://miracleformegan.wordpress.com

Made in the USA
San Bernardino, CA
08 December 2019